BLACKSTONE

FAMILY MAGIC SHOPPE

Published by Ideals Children's Books
An imprint of Hambleton-Hill Publishing, Inc.
Nashville, Tennessee 37218

Printed and bound in the United States of America

ISBN 1-57102-300-3

Graphic Design/Art Direction
John Laughlin

Photography
Scott Bonner

Blackstone Magik Enterprises, Inc.
Licensor

Williams-Bell & Associates, Inc.
Packager

CARD MAGIC

The BLACKSTONE Family Magic Shoppe

By Charles Reynolds

Ideals Children's Books • Nashville, Tennessee
an imprint of Hambleton-Hill Publishing, Inc.

Card tricks are, without a doubt, the most popular type of magic. They can be performed on theater stages or in your own living room. Some of the greatest magicians of the twentieth century, including Howard Thurston and Harry Houdini, started their performing careers doing an act exclusively with cards. Card magic was always a great interest of my father's, the first Blackstone, as it is with me. Often the card tricks are as fondly remembered by audiences as the vanishing elephant or the lady sawed in two by the giant buzz saw.

When most of us think of card tricks the first words that enter our minds are "pick a card, any card." These are usually followed by "don't let me see it" and "put it back in the deck." This plot of finding a selected card is, indeed, the most common effect in card magic.

Once you know how to find the chosen card (how to "control" it in magicians' terms), you must then come up with a mystifying and entertaining way to reveal it. Every card trick has an *effect* (what the audience experiences) and a *method* (the secret means by which the illusion is accomplished). What is important to the audience is the *effect*. If you know a dozen ways to control a card and only one way to reveal it, you only know one card trick. But if you know one way to control a card (the audience is not aware of this secret anyway) and a dozen different ways to reveal it, then you know a dozen card tricks.

In this book, I will teach you how to control a card and some amazing ways to reveal it.

—Harry Blackstone Jr.

CARD

MAGiC

This simple trick will keep your friends guessing!

The secret to successful card magic is learning to control the cards. That is, when a card is picked and then returned to the deck, you must be able to control where that mystery card goes so that you can magically reveal it later. One way to control a card is with a *key card*.

A key card is a card that you have secretly chosen to end up next to the mystery card. When a key card is placed next to a mystery card, the deck can be cut any number of times without changing the order of the cards. In fact, it will stay in that order until the deck is shuffled. There are two basic kinds of key cards: the *top key card* and the *bottom key card*.

Using a Top Key Card

1. Secretly look at the top card of the deck.

2. Ask someone in your audience to pick a card from the deck and look at it. Tell him not to let you see it (*Figure 1*).

3. Tell him to place the card on top of the deck (on top of your key card), reminding him to remember his card (*Figure 2*).

4. Cut the deck (*Figure 3*). The mystery card will still be on top of your key card. Cut the deck as many times as you wish to make the trick seem even more incredible.

5. Spread the deck faceup, from left to right (*Figure 4*). *(Note: In order for the tricks in this book to work, you must always spread the deck from left to right.)*

6. Casually look over the cards and find your key card. The mystery card will be to the *left* of your key card (*Figures 4 & 5*).

Practice your tricks until you are perfectly comfortable performing them.

Figure 1

Figure 2

Figure 3

Figure 4

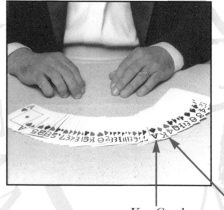

Figure 5

Key Card   Mystery Card

Using a Bottom Key Card

1. Secretly look at the bottom card of the deck.

2. Then follow steps 2 through 5 for using a Top Key Card.

The difference now is that the mystery card will be *below* your key card, and, when the cards are spread out left to right, the mystery card will be to the *right* of the key card.

Never reveal the secrets behind your tricks.

These three simple exercises will help you understand how the key card works.

Exercise I

Put each of the suits of the deck in order, Ace through King. Stack the four suits together. Look at the deck faceup and then cut it. The top and bottom cards change, but all the other cards are in the same order. Cut the deck again. The top and bottom cards are next to one another again, and the order of the deck still has not changed.

Exercise II: The Top Key Card

Look at the top card of the deck. This card will be your key card (let's make it the Ace of Spades, *Figure 1*). Have a card selected (let's make this card the King of Diamonds—the "mystery" card, *Figure 2*) and placed on top of the deck. Cut the deck several times then spread it faceup, from left to right. The King of Diamonds is now just to the left of the Ace of Spades—your key card (*Figure 3*). This will not change, no matter how many times the deck is cut.

Exercise III: The Bottom Key Card

Look at the bottom card of the deck. This card will be your key card (let's make it the Ace of Spades). Have a card selected (let's make this card the King of Diamonds) and placed on top of the deck. Cut the deck several times. The King of Diamonds will stay just below the Ace of Spades—your key card. Spread the deck faceup, from left to right. The King of Diamonds is now just to the right of the Ace of Spades (*Figure 4*). No matter how many times you cut the deck, this will not change.

You now possess one of the most powerful secrets of card magic! With this secret alone, you can convince people that you are a highly skilled card magician. Everyone will ask, "How did you do that?"

Adding a simple wave of a magic wand can greatly add to the professional look of your performance.

Figure 1

Figure 2

Figure 3

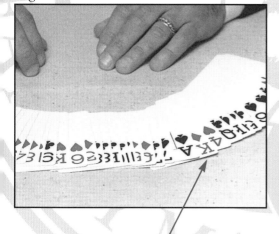

Mystery Card is left of Key Card

Figure 4

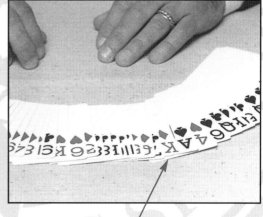

Mystery Card is right of Key Card

Never perform the same trick twice in one show.

A special kind of shuffle used by all magicians.

1. Hold the deck facedown in your right hand. Your right forefinger should curl around the cards with its tip touching the top card. Your thumb should be on the bottom side of the deck and the remaining fingers on the top (*Figure 1*).

2. Hold your left hand in front of the deck, palm up. Then move the deck forward to your left hand. Let a small packet fall from the top of the deck into your left hand (*Figure 2*).

3. Let another small packet fall from your right hand on top of the packet already in your left hand. Keep doing this until there is only a small packet remaining in your right hand. Then drop this packet on top of the cards in your left hand (*Figure 3*).

Using the Hindu Shuffle with a Bottom Key Card

1. Shuffle the deck and secretly look at the bottom card (let's make this card the Ace of Spades, *Figure 4*).

2. Fan the cards out in your hands and ask someone to pick a card from the center of the deck (*Figure 5*).

3. After a card has been selected, simply begin to Hindu Shuffle the cards into your left hand (*Figures 1 through 4*).

4. Tell your spectator to drop her card in the deck at any time as you are shuffling (*Figure 6*).

5. When her card is placed on the cards in your left hand, simply drop the remaining cards in your right hand on top of it (*Figure 7*). Now, your key card will be directly on top of the mystery card—exactly where you want it to be. You can reveal it any number of ways.

In magic, magnetism *pertains to telepathy, clairvoyance, and other areas in which the mind can perform amazing feats!*

Figure 1

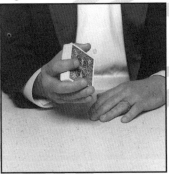

Figure 2

Figure 3

Figure 4

Figure 5

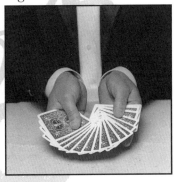

Figure 6

Figure 7

The phrase "Hocus Pocus" is believed to have originated with Italian performers who called upon "Ochus Bochus," a wizard, to aid them in their magical endeavors.

The Overhand Shuffle

1. Hold the deck in your left hand with the top of the deck toward your thumb (*Figure 1*).

2. With your right hand, remove about half of the deck from the bottom of the stack in your left hand (*Figure 2*). Then shuffle them on top of the cards in your left hand (*Figure 3*).

Figure 1

Figure 2

Figure 3

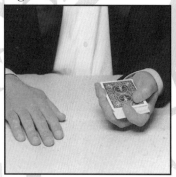

The False Overhand Shuffle

This shuffle allows you to keep your bottom key card in place while appearing to shuffle the deck.

1. Hold the deck in your left hand, just as in the regular overhand shuffle (*Figure 4*).

2. With your right hand, take a packet of cards from the *center* of the deck, leaving a few cards on the bottom of the packet in your left hand (*Figure 5*).

3. Shuffle the cards in the right hand to the top of the left-hand packet as you would normally do (*Figure 6*). Be careful not to disturb the bottom key card. When you do this simple false shuffle, do not call attention to the cards by looking at them.

Richard Potter was the first American magician to prove his abilities successfully in his native country.

Figure 4

Figure 5

Figure 6

1. Hold the deck facedown in your left hand with your thumb at the left side, fingers at the right side, and forefinger curled over the front.

2. Arch your right hand over the deck, as if you were going to pick it up in that hand (*Figure 7*). As you do, push the top card to the right so that it pivots on your right little finger. Keep your hand curved and your fingers together.

3. Bend your fingers and take the card in your right palm (*Figures 8 & 9*). You must do this when the audience's attention is elsewhere. Above all, do not look at your hand as the palming is taking place.

Figure 7

Figure 8

Figure 9

Martin Van Buren, the eighth president of the United States, was named "The Little Magician" due to his political maneuvering.

Magically locate the mystery card using a top key card.

1. Give the deck of cards to someone in your audience, and ask him to shuffle them.

2. Say to your audience, *"I can read a person's mind simply by feeling his pulse."*

3. Take the deck and spread it faceup in your hands to show that it is well mixed (*Figure 1*). As you do, casually look at the top card (the card farthest left in your hand). This will be your key card.

4. Spread the deck facedown on the table (*Figure 2*). Ask someone to choose a card from the center of the spread. Turn your head away as he takes the card.

5. Square the deck and remind the person to remember his card (*Figure 3*).

6. Have the person place the card on top of the deck (*Figure 4*) and then cut the deck. (This will place his card just above your key card.) Cut the deck twice more.

7. Spread the deck faceup on the table, from left to right (*Figure 5*). Don't look at the deck yet! Talk about your amazing "pulse reading" abilities. Have the person put out his hand, then take his wrist as if you were taking his pulse. Slowly pass his hand along the spread-out deck.

9. Now look for your key card. The mystery card will be just to the left of it (*Figure 6*). (In this example, the Ace of Spades is the key card, and the King of Diamonds is the mystery card.)

10. Add excitement to your act by closing your eyes and pretending to concentrate very hard. Push some cards to the side and say that his card isn't among them. Pass his hand back and forth over the deck. Keep pushing away more cards until the only one left is his card. Pretend to be exhausted by all the "concentrating" you have done to "read" his pulse.

Magicians have been called the scientists of show business.

Figure 1

Figure 2

Figure 3

Figure 4

Figure 5

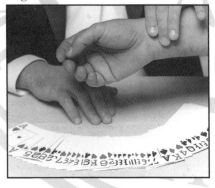

Figure 6

Mystery Card is left of Key Card

Of all the senses, hearing is the easiest to trick.

Surprise your audience by making them think you can't find the mystery card!

1. Give the deck an overhand shuffle (see page 14).

2. Have someone choose a card from the middle of the deck and show it to the audience while you look away. As she does this, secretly look at the bottom card of the deck in your hand.

3. Hold the deck in your left hand (*Figure 1*). With your right hand, cut off the bottom half of the deck and hold it in your right hand (*Figure 2*). Then, with your left hand, hold out the top half of the deck and tell the person to place her card on top of it (*Figure 3*).

4. Drop the cards in your right hand on top (*Figure 4*). Your key card will now be directly on top of the mystery card.

5. Cut the deck two or three times.

6. Explain that you will deal through the deck and magically find her mystery card.

7. Hold the deck facedown in your left hand. With your right hand, start dealing cards faceup on the table (*Figure 5*).

8. When you come to the key card, the next card will be the mystery card, but don't stop dealing. Simply note what her card is and continue to deal five or six more cards.

9. Suddenly stop dealing and announce, *"The next card I turn over will be your card!"* Your audience will think you have failed because the mystery card is already on the table.

10. Now slowly reach down and turn her mystery card facedown (*Figure 6*).

Natural magic *refers to things in nature that are difficult to explain. For example, a glass disk can make close-up objects appear far away.*

Figure 1

Figure 2

Figure 3

Figure 4

Figure 5

Figure 6

A curved object, such as a clear glass, can be used as a lens to refract light and reverse an image.

In magic you don't always have to look for a card; sometimes you can just listen for it.

1. Shuffle the deck and secretly look at the bottom card. This will be your key card.

2. Have someone select a card and look at it (*Figure 1*).

3. Ask him to place the card on top of the deck (*Figure 2*). Cut the cards.

4. Have someone cut the deck twice more and then place it facedown on the table (*Figure 3*).

5. Explain that, through long study and practice, you have become sensitive to the tones of a person's voice. You have discovered that if a person calls out the name of each card, you will be able to tell which one is his card by the change in his voice.

6. Ask the person to deal the cards faceup on to the table, one at time, calling out the name of each one.

7. Pretend to concentrate very hard on each card. For added drama, have the person repeat the name of a card. Then say, *"No, that's not it. Go on."*

8. When you hear the name of your key card called, the next card will be his mystery card. When the name of the mystery card is called, dramatically call out, *"Stop! I can tell from the tone of your voice that that is your card."*

Place a single sheet of newspaper against a wall and rub it with a wool cloth. Now step back and watch! The newspaper will remain stuck to the wall.

Figure 1

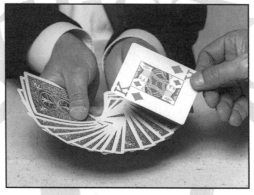

Figure 2

Figure 3

Rub a balloon against your hair. Now place it against a wall and watch it stick! Magic? No! The balloon was given an electric charge.

Mystify your audience by having the mystery card revealed— by someone who isn't even there!

1. Before you begin this trick, ask a friend to help. This friend should wait by the telephone and should already know what the key card will be. Arrange to put this key card on the bottom of the deck.

2. Start the trick by giving the deck a False Overhand Shuffle (see page 14), keeping the bottom card in place.

3. Fan the cards out in your hands and have someone select a card. Tell her to look at it and remember it.

4. Then ask her to place the card on top of the deck. Cut the cards.

5. Give the phone number of your friend to the person and ask her to call. Explain that your friend will magically name her mystery card over the phone.

6. Then have the person deal the cards from the top of the deck, one at a time, calling out the name of each one to your friend on the phone. Your friend then simply listens for the prearranged key card and on the next card calls, *"STOP!"*

John Henry Anderson, a Scottish magician, was touted as "The Great Wizard of the North."

Use a secret code to reveal the mystery card.

1. Shuffle the deck and secretly look at the bottom card.

2. Have someone select a card and look at it.

3. Ask him to place the card on the top of the deck. Cut the cards.

4. Spread the deck faceup on the table, from left to right, as if to show that it is well mixed.

5. Secretly look for your key card. The mystery card will be just to the *left* of the key card. Don't tell anyone that you know what the mystery card is.

6. Explain that you have a friend with remarkable mind-reading abilities who can tune in on a person's thoughts and name the card he chose. (Remember to let your friend know when you are going to call.)

7. Call your friend. When she hears your voice, she will repeat to you the suits of the deck, pausing between each one, *"Clubs...Hearts... Spades...Diamonds."* When she names the suit of the mystery card, let us say, *"Hearts,"* you say, *"Just a minute."* She now knows that the card is a Heart.

8. Now she begins calling out the values, Ace through King. When she calls out the value of the mystery card, for example, *"Five,"* you say, *"I'd like you to speak to my friend."* She now knows that the mystery card is the Five of Hearts.

9. Hand the phone to the spectator who explains to your friend the nature of the experiment. Your friend, with suitable dramatics, then "reads the spectator's mind" and tells what the card is. Remember, you are not supposed to even know what the card is, so the idea that someone on the other end of a phone line could know it seems to be a total impossibility.

October 31 has been set aside as National Magic Day in commemoration of the day Harry Houdini died.

"Force" your audience to pick the card you want.

1. Before beginning the trick, you and your friend (whom you will call) must know the top card of the deck.

2. As you start the trick, give the deck a false shuffle, keeping the top card in place. This is done by turning the deck faceup and using the False Overhand Shuffle (see page 14).

3. Place the deck facedown on the table.

4. Ask someone to take off a pile of cards from the top of the deck and place it on the table.

5. Pick up the bottom portion of the deck and place it crosswise on the other pile (*Figure 1*). Do this casually while you are talking to the person.

6. Talk to the person about your friend with remarkable mind-reading powers. Show her a piece of paper with your friend's telephone number on it. Do not pay any attention to the cut deck.

7. Lift the top portion of the deck. Point to the top card of the bottom portion (*Figure 2*) and tell the person to look at her card. Actually, this is the original top card of the deck, but the person's attention has been on other things and the cut deck has been forgotten. (Magicians call this a "force.")

8. Have the spectator call your friend who then goes into her mind-reading act. Finally, after much concentration, she will name the card in as impressive a manner as she can manage.

Alexander Herrmann, also known as "Herrmann the Great," once pulled a cigar from the whiskers of President Ulysses S. Grant.

Figure 1

Figure 2

The mystery card escapes from its box–just like Houdini!

1. Begin by removing the deck from its box. Ask someone to shuffle the cards, then take them back (*Figure 1*).

2. Tell a story about how Houdini, the great magician and escape artist, escaped from a locked trunk.

3. As you are talking, hold the deck in your left hand and bring your right hand over it (*Figure 2*). With your right thumb, bend back the left corner of the bottom card. Keep talking as you do this. Don't look at your hands!

4. Ask someone to select a card, and then replace it using the Hindu Shuffle (see page 12). Now the bent key card will be above the mystery card. Be sure to keep the bent corner of the key card hidden by your hand.

5. Cut the deck at the bent key card so that the bent key card goes to the bottom of the deck. The mystery card will now be on top of the deck.

6. Pick up the deck and place it into the box. The top of the deck (where the mystery card is located) must go into the box toward the side where the flap tucks in. This is the side of the box with the half-circle cutout.

7. Close the box, and (without the audience seeing) tuck the box flap in between the top (mystery) card and the rest of the deck (*Figure 3*). Hold your thumb over the half-circle cutout to hide the card (*Figure 4*). Explain how Houdini was locked inside a trunk that was placed out of sight inside a curtained cabinet.

8. Place the deck behind your back and hold it in one hand (*Figure 5*). Then, using your thumb, contact the card at the half-circle opening and pull it out about an inch.

9. Now ask the name of the mystery card. Quickly reach behind your back and pull out the card. Then bring out the deck still sealed in its box. Houdini has made his escape!

Figure 1

Figure 2

Figure 3

Figure 4

Figure 5

Talk to your audience while you are doing your secret maneuvering—tell a story or a joke.

Use a Detective Card to track down the mystery card.

1. Before beginning, secretly reverse a card—any of the Sevens—at a position seven cards from the bottom of the deck (*Figure 1*). You should then have six facedown cards on the bottom of the deck, then the faceup Seven, and then the rest of the deck. (The Seven is called a *remote key card.*)

2. Start the trick by fanning the deck facedown in your hands. Be sure not to reveal the faceup Seven. Ask someone to select a card (*Figure 2*).

3. Have the card replaced using the Hindu Shuffle (see page 12). The reversed Seven is now exactly seven cards above the mystery card.

4. Square up the deck and place it facedown on the table (*Figure 3*).

5. Explain to the audience that a Detective Card is a special card that finds other cards. Spread the deck facedown on the table (*Figure 4*), revealing the reversed Seven in the middle. Then say, *"For example, the Detective Card in this deck is the Seven."*

6. Cut the spread so that the Seven is brought to the top of the deck (*Figure 5*). Be sure not to change the order of the cards when you do this.

7. Explain that the Detective Card, the Seven, tells you that the mystery card is seven cards down in the deck. Toss the Seven on the table and hand the deck to the person who chose the mystery card.

8. Have her count down seven cards where the mystery card will be miraculously found!

It is important to direct your audience's attention in another direction while you execute a sleight-of-hand movement.

Figure 1

Figure 2

Figure 3

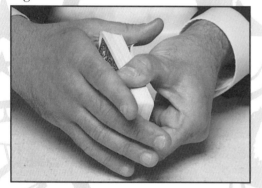

Figure 4

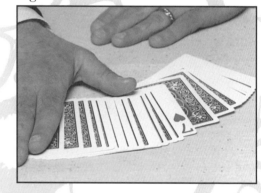

Figure 5

Magicians often make their movements familiar ones so that the audience will rely on previous experiences and will not notice their sleight-of-hand movements.

Use a magic word to find the mystery card.

1. To prepare for this trick, have the bent key card placed twelve cards up from the bottom of the deck (*Figure 1*).

2. Begin the trick with a False Overhand Shuffle (see page 14). (Be sure that the packet of cards you pull out to shuffle is above your set up of twelve cards on the bottom of the deck.)

3. Have someone choose a card from the middle of the deck (*Figure 2*). Make sure the person does not take a card out of the bottom twelve cards.

4. Replace the cards using the Hindu Shuffle (see page 12), so that the stack with the bent key card is dropped on top of the mystery card.

5. Cut the deck at the bent key card so that the bent key card ends up on the bottom (*Figure 3*). The mystery card is now twelve cards down in the deck.

6. Explain to the person that this trick works with the magic word, "abracadabra."

7. Give the deck to him and ask him to spell "abracadabra," placing a card on the table for each letter. Spell along with him just to make sure that the word is spelled correctly. After he has spelled "abracadabra" (which has eleven letters), have him turn over the next card. It will be his mystery card.

What direction would you drive to get from Reno to Los Angeles? Southeast, of course. Reno is west of L.A.!

Figure 1

Figure 2

Bent Key Card

Figure 3

Which state extends farther south than the rest of the United States? You guessed it—Hawaii!

Magically deal your way to the mystery card.

1. Before you prepare for this trick, place your bent key card 22 cards up from the bottom of the deck (31 cards from the top) (*Figure 1*).

2. To begin, spread out the top part of the deck (the part above the bent key card) and have someone choose a card (*Figure 2*).

3. Have the card replaced using the Hindu Shuffle (see page 12). Do this shuffle slowly and be sure the card is put back before you get to the bent key card. If you are close to shuffling down to the bent key card, simply stop and extend the cards in your left hand saying, *"Place your card back in the deck"* (*Figure 3*).

4. After the card has been replaced, cut the deck several times. On the last time, cut the deck just below the bent key card so that it ends up on the bottom. This will place the mystery card 22 cards down in the deck, the proper place for the dealing that is to follow.

5. Deal the deck into two piles, one to the spectator and one to yourself (*Figure 4*). Make sure the first card dealt goes to the spectator. When the cards are all dealt, ask her to look through her cards for the one she chose. She will not find it.

6. Say, *"It must be in my pile."* Pick up your pile of cards and deal again (remember, the first card goes to her). Have her look for the card, but again she will not find it.

7. Continue dealing the cards as in Step 5, and each time she will not find her card. Finally, she will be left with two cards, and you will have one in front of you. Neither of her last two cards will be the mystery card.

8. Ask her the name of her card. Then dramatically turn over your card— the mystery card.

NOTE: This trick must be done with a full deck of 52 cards.

John Henry Anderson chose some unusual places to post his playbills—such as the side of a pyramid in Egypt and on the cliffs of Niagra Falls in the United States.

Figure 1

Bent Key Card

Figure 2

Figure 3

Figure 4

Tell someone that you can put a half-dollar into a pop bottle. Once they tell you it can't be done, take a dollar bill, tear it in half, fold it, and put it in the bottle.

Use a force card to help you "predict" what the mystery card will be.

1. To prepare for this trick, secretly set up the deck so that the top card is facedown, the second card is faceup, the third card is facedown (remember the name of this card), and the fourth card is faceup (*Figure 1*). Use a deck with a white border in its back design so any card that is secretly reversed will not show up if the deck is spread slightly.

2. Turn the deck faceup and spread the cards to show that they are well mixed (*Figure 2*). Do not spread all the way to the top of the deck where the reversed cards are.

3. With the deck still faceup, give the cards a False Overhand Shuffle (see page 14). Be sure to keep your four set-up cards in place.

4. Turn the deck facedown and hand it to a spectator to hold behind his back.

5. Tell your audience that you are going to make a prediction about the cards. Then take a piece of paper and write the name of the third card (*Figure 3*). Place the prediction facedown on the table.

6. Tell the person to take the top card of the deck and push it somewhere into the center of the deck (*Figure 4*). He must keep the cards behind his back.

7. Then tell him to take the bottom card and push it into the center of the deck. (This is just to confuse the person.)

8. Now tell him to turn the top card faceup and push it into the center of the deck. (This card is already faceup, so now it will be facedown. When it is pushed in with the other facedown cards, it will be lost.)

Adelaide Herrmann, widow of "Herrmann the Great," was one of the world's most famous female magicians.

9. Tell him to cut the deck three times. Explain that one card has been turned faceup in the deck and that it is face to face with another card. Explain that there is no possible way that you could know what card it would be placed next to because he could have put it anywhere in the deck.

10. Have him bring the deck forward. Spread it out on the table.

11. Point out the faceup card (*Figure 5*) and remove the card that is face to face with it. Now show your prediction and watch the look of amazement as you turn the card over—the predicted card!

Figure 1

Figure 2

Figure 3

Figure 4

Figure 5

Ehrich Weiss became "Houdini" by simply adding an "i" to well-known magician Jean-Eugène Robert-Houdin's last name.

Your audience will think the trick is over,
but the surprise ending will add to their amazement!

1. Before the trick, secretly set up the deck with 12 red cards on top and, just under them, two black cards of the same value, for example, two black Sevens.

2. Turn the deck faceup and do a False Overhand Shuffle (see page 14), leaving the top 14 cards in place.

3. Turn the deck facedown and deal off two facedown piles of seven cards each (*Figure 1*). The first pile should be dealt to the other person. She will now have a pile of seven red cards, and you will have a pile of five red cards with two black cards on top.

4. Explain to the person that she is to do exactly as you do and, if she does, amazing things will happen.

5. Both you and the spectator hold the packets of cards behind you. Say, *"I'll mix my cards and you mix yours."* (Actually, you just pretend to mix yours so that the two black Sevens stay on top.)

6. Then say, *"Now, remove a card from the center of your packet, and I will do the same. Bring it out from behind your back, but don't look at it. I'll do the same."* (Actually, you bring out the top card of your packet—a black Seven—and she brings out any one of her cards which will, of course, be red.

7. Say, *"You take my card, and I'll take yours. Put the card behind your back, turn it over so that it is faceup, and place it into the center of your packet. I'll do the same."* (Actually, you take her card but do not turn it over. Instead, place it facedown into the center of your packet. Then take the top card of your packet—the second black Seven—turn it faceup, and put it into the center of your packet.)

Harry Blackstone, Sr. and his brother Pete created a vaudeville act called "Harry Bouton & Co., Straight and Crooked Magic."

8. Say, *"Bring your packet forward and let's see if the magic has worked."* Spread your two packets showing the two matching faceup cards. Say, *"The magic worked, we both chose black Sevens!"*

9. Turn the two packets over showing that all the other cards are red. Then say, *"What's even more amazing is that they were the only two black cards."*

Figure 1

Figure 2

Figure 3

Finding the mystery card is twice as amazing when you use two decks.

* For this trick, you will need two decks of cards with contrasting back colors, for example, one with blue backs and one with red. (Or, you can use two decks with different backgrounds.)

1. Show the two decks of cards with contrasting backs (*Figure 1*).

2. Allow an audience member to choose either deck, and you take the other one (*Figure 2*). Explain that the theme of this trick is *"Do As I Do,"* and that it is very important that both of you do exactly the same thing.

3. Shuffle your deck. The person shuffles his deck.

4. After you have finished your shuffle, secretly look at and remember the bottom card of your deck. This will be your key card. The person should not know that you have done this.

5. Switch decks with the person.

6. Remove a card from the center of your deck, look at it, and place it on top of your deck (*Figure 3*). Have him do the same.

7. Cut your deck three times and have him do the same.

8. Switch decks again. Tell the person to look through his deck and remove the card he chose and you will do the same. What you actually do is look for the key card. Directly below it will be his chosen card, and that is the card you remove and place facedown on the table. The person, imitating your actions exactly, removes the same card and places it facedown on the table.

9. Turn over both cards to show that they match!

At the height of his career, Harry Houdini was one of the highest paid performers in show business.

Figure 1

Figure 2

Figure 3

Harry Houdini was known as the
"Handcuff King and Escape Artist."

Use this sleight-of-hand trick to baffle your friends.

1. Shuffle the deck of cards and have someone select a card. Remove the top half of the deck and have her place her card on top of the bottom stack of cards (*Figure 1*).

2. Place the top part of the deck on top of her mystery card, but turn it faceup (*Figure 2*).

3. Hold the deck in your left hand. With your left thumb, push a few cards off into your right hand. Hold these cards in your right hand so that your thumb is on top and your fingers are underneath (*Figure 3*).

4. Now, turn the right-hand packet over so that it is facedown by turning your right hand toward yourself. Now your fingers will be on top and your thumb underneath.

5. Immediately push a few more cards off the left-hand packet and take them faceup *under* the facedown packet in your right hand (*Figure 4*). Your right thumb holds them in place.

6. Turn your right hand over again (so that your thumb is on top, fingers underneath). With your left thumb, push a few more cards off the left-hand packet. Take them under the right-hand packet where your fingers hold them in place.

7. Continue Steps 4, 5, and 6 until you come to the break in the deck where the mystery card was placed—it will be the first facedown card. (Do this quickly so that the audience will think you are mixing the cards faceup and facedown. Actually, you'll end up with two packets of cards, one facedown and one faceup.)

8. When you reach the mystery card, push it under the bottom, faceup card in your right hand and hold it there. At the same time, flip over the packet of cards in your *left* hand so that they are faceup. Push off a few cards from the left-hand packet and take them under the right-hand packet.

David Kotkin borrowed his stage name from the hero of Charles Dickens' David Copperfield.

9. Now continue Steps 4, 5, and 6 as before.

10. When you run out of cards in your left hand, your right hand will be holding a deck with the bottom half faceup and top half facedown (*Figure 5*). Spread the cards to the point where the halves are face to face and turn the top half over. Now all the cards are faceup except the mystery card.

11. Spread the deck faceup on the table (*Figure 6*), showing that one card is facedown. Ask the person to name her card. Turn over the facedown card, showing that it is her card.

Figure 1

Figure 2

Figure 3

Figure 4

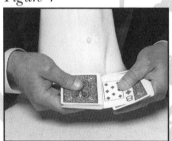

Figure 5

Figure 6

David Copperfield is the first magician to have his name placed on the Hollywood Walk of Fame during his lifetime.

Combine the techniques of the key card and the forced card to convince a person that you can read his mind.

1. Before you begin this trick, secretly set up two cards on the bottom of the deck. Remember the names of these cards. The bottom card you will force and the card just above it is your key card. For example, let us say that the bottom card is the King of Diamonds and that the card above it is the Ace of Spades.

2. You will now force the bottom card, using the Hindu Shuffle (see page 12). Your force card remains on the bottom packet in your right hand.

3. As the cards from your right-hand packet fall into your left hand (*Figure 1*), say to the spectator, *"Tell me when to stop."* When he stops you, look him straight in the eyes and say, *"Right there?"* Then tilt the packet in your right hand toward him, showing him the bottom card, and say, *"Look at the card you stopped at"* (*Figure 2*).

4. Drop the cards in your right hand on top of those in your left (*Figure 3*). Say, *"Please don't forget your card."* (Forcing a card this way may seem too obvious to you, but if you do it with confidence your audience will never question it.)

5. Now tell the spectator that after many years of practice, you have developed an amazing ability—you can tell if a person is lying just by the tone of his voice. Then say, *"I can prove it."*

6. Give the person the deck and have him deal the cards faceup on the table as you turn away. Tell him to call out the name of each card as he deals it, but, when he comes to his chosen card, tell him to lie and call out the name of another card.

7. Keep your back to him but listen for the Ace of Spades (your key card). When he calls out the name of the next card, he will be lying. Dramatically yell, *"Stop! I know by the tone of your voice that you're not telling the truth."*

Several pieces of Harry Houdini's collection of props can be found in the Library of Congress in Washington, D.C.

8. Then say that you will go one step further by reading his mind and telling him what his card really is. In your best dramatic fashion, tell him it is the King of Diamonds. (Remember, you know the card because you forced it on him using the Hindu Shuffle.)

Figure 1

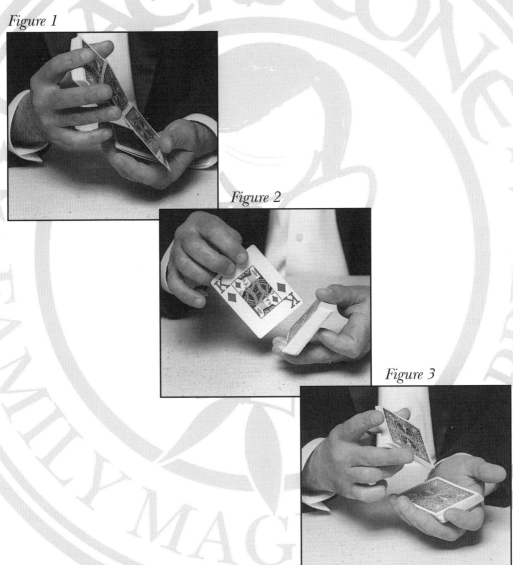

Figure 2

Figure 3

Use this mathematical force to convince your audience that they are witnessing the "science" of numerology at work.

1. Shuffle the deck and spread the cards from left to right to show they are well mixed. As you are doing this, secretly spot the card that is ten down from the top (left side) of the deck (*Figure 1*).

2. Square the deck (*Figure 2*) and say, *"Many card tricks work by sleight of hand. Others work by pure magic. But this one works by numerology, which is the science of predicting the future by numbers. I will now make a prediction."* Take a piece of paper and write the name of the card that is 10 down from the top of the deck. Don't let anyone see what you write (*Figure 3*).

3. *"In numerology,"* you explain, *"all numbers are reduced to one number. I will demonstrate. Please give me a number between 10 and 20."*

4. When someone gives you a number, for example 14, count that number of cards facedown on the table from the top of the deck.

5. Then say, *"The number you have chosen consists of two digits, a one and a four, so using numerology, we will reduce it to one number. One plus four makes five."* Count four cards back on top of the deck and place the fifth card to one side. Turn away as she looks at the card and shows it to several other people. This is the force card that you have predicted on the slip of paper.

6. Put the card back on top of the deck and drop the remaining cards you have counted on top of that (*Figure 4*). (This places the force card 10 down from the top again.)

7. Pick up the deck and fan it faceup (*Figure 5*). Ask another person to name a number between 10 and 20. Hand the deck to that person and ask him to count that number of cards on to the table. Add the digits together and count down to that card in the pile that was dealt. Place that card facedown to the side and ask someone to hold it, "so it doesn't get away."

The main street in Colon, Michigan, where Harry Blackstone, Sr. is buried, has been renamed after him.

8. Ask the first person what her card was and ask her to read your "numerological prediction" from the piece of paper. You have correctly predicted her card.

9. Finally, ask the other person to turn over his card. It's the same card!

Figure 1

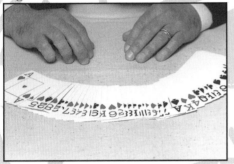

Figure 2

Figure 3

Figure 4

Figure 5

Jean-Eugène Robert-Houdin explained that a magician is an actor who plays the role of a man who can work miracles.

This trick requires misdirection, *which means getting your audience to look in the wrong place at the right time.*

1. Ask someone to think of an hour of the day from 1 through 12. It should be the complete hour, not 11:45 or 2:15.

2. Have the deck shuffled and handed back to you.

3. Explain that you will remove cards, one at a time faceup, from the top of the deck. Tell her to remember the card that falls at her number. Begin dealing cards from the top, calling out each number from 1 through 12.

4. Put the cards back on top of the deck. Then place the deck behind your back and ask the person to concentrate on her card. *"I think I've got it,"* you say as your hand emerges from behind your back with one card, which you put in your pocket. (What really happens is you take any card from the center of the deck and place it in your pocket. Then you remove the card from the bottom of the deck and place it on the top. This, of course, places her card farther down in the deck than it was before.)

5. Bring the deck out from behind your back and ask what the hour of the day was at which her card fell. For example, let's say it was six o'clock. Deal five cards facedown on the table and the sixth card off to one side.

6. Turn over the five cards initially dealt on the table. Ask if her card is among them.

7. In the few seconds that she is looking at the cards, bring your hand over the deck in readiness to palm the top card (see page 15).

8. When the spectator sees that her card is not among the five cards, ask her to turn over the sixth card. At the instant that is done, palm the top card of the deck and put your hand (with the palmed card) in your pocket.

9. Remind her that you had put one card in your pocket. Now slowly withdraw the palmed card, which will be her card.

Harry Blackstone, Jr. originally planned to become a radio announcer.

Take a chance on making a match.

1. Have a friend shuffle the deck and then divide it into three piles in front of you.

2. Before you turn over the top card of each pile, say, *"I betcha there will be two cards of the same suit showing."* He will think, *"Four suits...only three cards...I shuffled the deck...how could I lose?"* So he will accept your challenge.

The Secret

Instead of trying to work out a formula for this trick, just say it backwards and see if *you* would take a chance on it. Turn over three cards and try to get three different suits without a match. Doesn't sound so good, does it? That's because it's a little more obvious that the chances are against you.

Ace, Two, Three . . .

Making a match is easy as can be.

1. Have a friend shuffle the deck, cut it, and then set it in front of you. Then say, *"As I deal these cards faceup on the table, I'll call out, 'Ace, two, three...and so on.' I betcha that I will correctly call out at least one card as I turn it over."*

2. Begin turning over one card at a time as you call out the *"Ace, two, three...."* After you have made a correct match, continue on through the deck. You'll probably find that others also match.

The Secret

The odds are in your favor for this one. You can find as many as six or seven matches in one run through the deck. Try it once for practice!

Harry Blackstone, Jr. worked as his father's assistant during school and college vacations.

This book is dedicated
to the memory of
Harry Blackstone, Jr.
1934 – 1997